ANYTHING YOU WANT

ANYTHING YOU WANT

///

40 Lessons for a New Kind of Entrepreneur

DEREK SIVERS
FOUNDER OF CD BABY

PORTFOLIO/PENGUIN

PORTFOLIO / PENGUIN

An imprint of Penguin Random House LLC
375 Hudson Street
New York, New York 10014
penguin.com

Portfolio / Penguin edition published 2015

First published by Do You Zoom, Inc. through The Domino Project

ISBN: 978-1-59184-826-4

Printed in the United States of America
3   5   7   9   10   8   6   4

Set in Garamond Premier Pro
Designed by Sabrina Boweres

Dedicated entirely to Seth Godin.
This book only exists because of his encouragement.

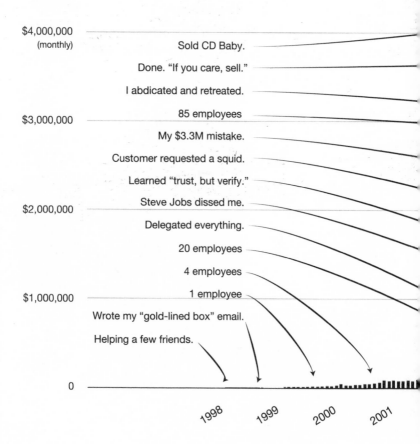

The growth of CD Baby, sales by month

$4,000,000 (monthly)	Sold CD Baby.
	Done. "If you care, sell."
	I abdicated and retreated.
$3,000,000	85 employees
	My $3.3M mistake.
	Customer requested a squid.
	Learned "trust, but verify."
$2,000,000	Steve Jobs dissed me.
	Delegated everything.
	20 employees
	4 employees
$1,000,000	1 employee
	Wrote my "gold-lined box" email.
	Helping a few friends.
0	

1998   1999   2000   2001

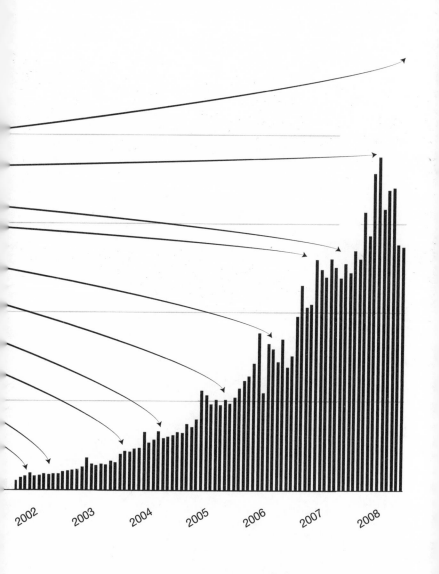

Ten years of experience in one hour

From 1998 to 2008, I had this wild experience of starting a little hobby, accidentally growing it into a big business, and then selling it for $22 million. So now people want to hear my thoughts.

People ask me about that experience, so I tell stories about how it went for me. Many of them are about all the things I did wrong. I made some horrible mistakes.

People ask my advice on how to approach situations in their lives or businesses, so I explain how I approach things. But my approach is just one way, and I could argue against it as well.

I'm not really suggesting that anyone should be like me. I'm pretty unusual, so what works for me might not work for others. But enough people thought that my stories and the philosophies I developed from this experience were worth sharing, so here we are.

This is most of what I learned in ten years, compacted into something you can read in an hour.

I hope you find these ideas useful for your own life or business. I also hope you disagree with some of them. Then I hope you e-mail me to tell me about your different point of view, because that's my favorite part of all. (I'm a student, not a guru.)

What's your compass?

Most people don't know why they're doing what they're doing. They imitate others, go with the flow, and follow paths without making their own. They spend decades in pursuit of something that someone convinced them they should want, without realizing that it won't make them happy.

Don't be on your deathbed someday, having squandered your one chance at life, full of regret because you pursued little distractions instead of big dreams. You need to know your personal philosophy of what makes you happy and what's worth doing.

In the following stories, you'll notice some common themes. These are my philosophies from the ten years I spent starting and growing a small business.

▶ Business is not about money. It's about making dreams come true for others and for yourself.

▶ Making a company is a great way to improve the world while improving yourself.

▶ When you make a company, you make a utopia. It's where you design your perfect world.

▶ Never do anything just for the money.

▶ Don't pursue business just for your own gain. Only answer the calls for help.

▶ Success comes from persistently improving and inventing, not from persistently promoting what's not working.

▶ Your business plan is moot. You don't know what people really want until you start doing it.

▶ Starting with no money is an advantage. You don't need money to start helping people.

▶ You can't please everyone, so proudly exclude people.

▶ Make yourself unnecessary to the running of your business.

▶ The real point of doing anything is to be happy, so do only what makes you happy.

What do these statements mean? What's the context? How are you supposed to apply them to your own situation?

Well . . . I don't love talking about myself, but for the lessons to make sense, I have to tell you my tale.

Just selling my CD

This story begins in 1997. I was a professional musician, age twenty-seven. I was making a full-time living just playing music—playing lots of gigs around the U.S. and Europe, producing people's records, playing on people's records, and running a little recording studio. I was even the musician and MC for a circus.

My bank account was always low, but never empty. I made enough money to buy a house in Woodstock, New York. I was living a musician's dream.

I made a CD of my music, and sold fifteen hundred copies at my concerts. I wanted to sell it online, but there were no businesses that would sell independent music online. Not one. I called up the big online record stores and they all told me the same thing: The only way I could get my CD into their online stores was through a major distributor.

Music distribution was an awful racket. Getting a distribution deal was as hard as getting a record deal. Distributors were notorious for taking thousands of CDs and paying you a year later, if ever. Record labels with deep pockets would buy expensive promotional placement, and the rest of us would just sit in the bin. If you didn't sell well in the first few months, you were kicked out of the system.

It's not that distributors were evil. It was just an awful

system, and I wanted nothing to do with it. So when the big online record stores told me they couldn't sell my CD directly, I thought, "Ah, screw it. I'll just set up my own online store. How hard could it be?"

But it was hard! In 1997, PayPal didn't exist, so I had to get a credit card merchant account, which cost $1,000 in setup fees and took three months of paperwork. The bank even had to send an inspector out to my location to make sure I was a valid business. Then I had to figure out how to build a shopping cart. I didn't know any programming, but I copied some examples from a programming book, with lots of trial and error.

Finally, though, I had a BUY NOW button on my website! In 1997 this was a big deal.

When I told my musician friends about my BUY NOW button, one friend asked, "Could you sell my CD, too?"

I thought about it for a minute and said, "Sure. No problem." I just did it as a favor. It took me a couple of hours to get him added into my system. I made a separate page for his CD on my band's website.

Then two other friends asked if I could sell their CDs. Then I started getting calls from strangers saying, "My friend Dave said you could sell my CD." The calls and e-mails kept coming. I said yes to all.

Two popular online music leaders announced it to their mailing lists. (Bryan Baker from Gajoob, and David Hooper. Thanks, guys!) Fifty more musicians signed up.

This was meant to be just a favor I was doing for a few friends. Hmmm . . .

Make a dream come true

Selling my friends' CDs was starting to take up a lot of my time. I realized I had accidentally started a business. But I didn't want to start a business! I was already living my dream life as a full-time musician. I didn't want anything to distract me from that.

So, I thought that by taking an unrealistically utopian approach, I could keep the business from growing too much. Instead of trying to make it big, I was going to make it small. It was the opposite of ambition, so I had to think in a way that was the opposite of ambitious.

I wrote down my utopian dream-come-true distribution deal from my musician's point of view. In a perfect world, my distributor would:

1. Pay me every week.

2. Show me the full name and address of everyone who bought my CD. (Because those are my fans, not the distributor's.)

3. Never kick me out for not selling enough. (Even if I sell only one CD every five years, it'll be there for someone to buy.)

4. Never allow paid placement. (Because it's not fair to those who can't afford it.)

That's it! That was my mission. I liked it. It was a worthy hobby. I named it CD Baby, and put my friends' CDs there.

Those four points were like a mission statement. I wrote them on the site, talked about them at every conference, and made sure everyone I worked with knew them.

The key point is that I wasn't trying to make a big business. I was just daydreaming about how one little thing would look in a perfect world.

When you make a business, you get to make a little universe where you control all the laws. This is your utopia.

When you make it a dream come true for yourself, it'll be a dream come true for someone else, too.

A business model with only two numbers

Like most people, I had no idea what to charge for my service. So I went to the record store in Woodstock, where they had some local musicians' CDs on the counter.

I asked the woman at the store, "How does it work if I sell my CD here?"

She said, "You set the selling price at whatever you want. We keep a flat $4 cut. And we pay you every week."

So I went home and wrote on my new cdbaby.com website, "You set the selling price at whatever you want. We keep a flat $4 cut. And we pay you every week." I figured if it worked for her, it was fine for me.

Because it was taking me about forty-five minutes of work to add a new album to the site, I also had to charge $25 per album as compensation for my time (shows you how much I thought my time was worth in those days). A few days later, I realized that $35 feels about the same as $25, so I bumped it up to $35 per album, which left me room to give discounts and still make a profit.

And that's it! Six years and $10 million later, those same two numbers were the sole source of income for the company: a $35 setup fee per album and a $4 cut per CD sold.

A business plan should never take more than a few hours of work—hopefully no more than a few minutes. The best plans start simple. A quick glance and common sense should tell you if the numbers will work. The rest are details.

This ain't no revolution

Five years after I started CD Baby, when it was a big success, the media said I had revolutionized the music business. But *revolution* is a term that people use only when you're successful. Before that, you're just a quirky person who does things differently.

People think a revolution needs to involve loud provocations, fists in the air, and bloodshed. But if you think true love looks like Romeo and Juliet, you'll overlook a great relationship that grows slowly. If you think your life's purpose needs to hit you like a lightning bolt, you'll overlook the little day-to-day things that fascinate you. If you think revolution needs to feel like war, you'll overlook the importance of simply serving people better.

When you're onto something great, it won't feel like revolution. It'll feel like uncommon sense.

If it's not a hit, switch

For the first time in my life, I had made something that people really wanted.

Before that, I had spent twelve years trying to promote my various projects—trying every marketing approach, networking, pitching, pushing. It always felt like an uphill battle, trying to open locked or slamming doors. I made progress, but only with massive effort.

But now . . . Wow! It was like I had written a hit song. A songwriter can write a hundred songs; then suddenly one of them really resonates with people and becomes a hit. Who knows why? It's not that it's necessarily better. But through some random set of circumstances or magic combination of ingredients, people love it.

Once you've got a hit, suddenly all the locked doors open wide. People love the hit so much that it seems to promote itself. Instead of trying to create demand, you're managing the huge demand.

So what's the lesson learned here?

We've all heard about the importance of persistence. But I had misunderstood. Success comes from persistently improving and inventing, not from persistently doing what's not working.

We all have lots of ideas, creations, and projects. When you present one to the world and it's not a hit, don't keep pushing it as is. Instead, get back to improving and inventing.

Present each new idea or improvement to the world. If multiple people are saying, "Wow! Yes! I need this! I'd be happy to pay you to do this!" then you should probably do it. But if the response is anything less, don't pursue it.

Don't waste years fighting uphill battles against locked doors. Improve or invent until you get that huge response.

No "yes."
Either "Hell yeah!"
or "no."

You can use this same rule on yourself if you're often overcommitted or too scattered. If you're not saying, *"Hell yeah!"* about something, say no. When deciding whether to do something, if you feel anything less than "Wow! That would be amazing! Absolutely! Hell yeah!" then say no.

When you say no to most things, you leave room in your life to throw yourself completely into that rare thing that makes you say, *"Hell yeah!"*

For every event you get invited to, every request to start a new project, if you're not saying, *"Hell yeah!"* about it, say no.

We're all busy. We've all taken on too much. Saying yes to less is the way out.

Just like that, my plan completely changed

When I first started CD Baby, I thought it was just a credit card processing service.

It was supposed to be a website that musicians would use to say, "Go here to buy my CD." Just click to buy, charge your card, and then go back to the musician's website. Kind of like PayPal, but this was two years before PayPal was invented.

The day I launched cdbaby.com, my second customer was a guy in the Netherlands. A week later he e-mailed to ask, "Any new releases?"

New releases? I didn't understand. I asked why he wanted to know which new people are using my service to charge credit cards.

He replied, "Oh, sorry; I thought it was a store."

A store? Oh! Interesting. He thinks I'm a store! I hadn't thought of that. Maybe if I set it up like a store, I'd actually be doing my friends a bigger favor, by getting total strangers to buy their music, too.

And just like that, my plan completely changed.

Five years later, when the iTunes Music Store launched, Apple asked us to be a digital distributor. I hadn't thought of that. But I said OK.

And just like that, my plan completely changed again.

Anytime you think you know what your new business will be doing, remember this quote from serial entrepreneur Steve Blank: "No business plan survives first contact with customers."

The advantage of no funding

Having no funding was a huge advantage for me.

A year after I started CD Baby, the dot-com boom happened. Anyone with a little hot air and a vague plan was given millions of dollars by investors. It was ridiculous.

Most business owners I knew would tell you about their businesses by talking about their second round of funding, their fancy encrypted replicated load-balancing database server, their twenty-person development team, their nice Midtown office with a pool table, and their weekly promotion parties. When you asked what the business actually did, they couldn't explain it clearly. Then they would talk about LOI, ROI, NDAs, IPOs, and all kinds of things that also had nothing to do with actually helping people.

I'm so glad I didn't have investors. I didn't have to please anybody but my customers and myself. No effort was spent on anything but my customers.

I'd get weekly calls from investment firms, wanting to invest in CD Baby. My immediate answer was always, "No thanks."

They'd say, "Don't you want to expand?"

I'd say, "No. I want my business to be smaller, not bigger." That always ended the conversation.

By not having any money to waste, you never waste money. Since I couldn't afford a programmer, I went to the bookstore and got a $25 book on PHP and MySQL programming. Then I sat down and learned it, with no programming experience. Necessity is a great teacher.

Even years later, the desks were just planks of wood on cinder blocks from the hardware store. I made the office computers myself from parts. My well-funded friends would spend $100,000 to buy something that I made myself for $1,000. They did it saying, "We need the very best," but it didn't improve anything for the customers.

Never forget that absolutely everything you do is for your customers. Make every decision—even decisions about whether to expand the business, raise money, or promote someone—according to what's best for your customers. If you're ever unsure what to prioritize, just ask your customers the open-ended question, "How can I best help you now?" Then focus on satisfying those requests.

None of your customers will ask you to turn your attention to expanding. They want you to keep your attention focused on them. It's counterintuitive, but the way to grow your business is to focus entirely on your existing customers. Just thrill them, and they'll tell everyone.

Start now.
No funding needed.

Watch out when anyone (including you) says he wants to do something big, but can't until he raises money. It usually means the person is more in love with the idea of being big-big-big than with actually doing something useful. For an idea to get big-big-big, it has to be useful. And being useful doesn't need funding.

If you want to be useful, you can always start now, with only 1 percent of what you have in your grand vision. It'll be a humble prototype version of your grand vision, but you'll be in the game. You'll be ahead of the rest, because you actually started, while others are waiting for the finish line to magically appear at the starting line.

For example, let's say you have a vision of making an international chain of enlightened modern schools. You picture it as a huge, world-changing organization, with hundreds of employees, dozens of offices, and expensive technology. But instead of waiting for that, you start by teaching somebody something this week. Find someone who will pay to learn something, meet her anywhere, and begin. It will be nothing but you, a student, and a notebook, but you'll be in business, and you can grow it from there.

If you want to make a movie recommendation service, start by telling friends to call you for movie recommendations. When you find a movie your friends like, they buy you a drink. Keep track of what you recommended and how your friends liked it, and improve from there.

Want to start a new airline? Next time you're at the airport when a flight is canceled, tell everyone at the gate that you'll lease a small plane to fly to their destination if they will split the costs. (This is how Richard Branson started Virgin Atlantic Airways.)

Starting small puts 100 percent of your energy into actually solving real problems for real people. It gives you a stronger foundation to grow from. It eliminates the friction of big infrastructure and gets right to the point. And it will let you change your plan in an instant, as you're working closely with those first customers telling you what they really need.

Since I had already built a website for my own CD, the first version of CD Baby took me only a few days to make, and it did almost nothing. It was a list of a few CDs, each with a BUY NOW button. Clicking that would put the CD in your cart and ask for your info. When you entered your info, the site would e-mail it to me.

That's it. For the first year, that's all the site did, and that's all it needed to do to become profitable.

I spent only $500 to start CD Baby. The first month, I earned back $300. But the second month I made $700, and it's been profitable every month since.

So no, your idea doesn't need funding to start. (You also don't need an MBA, a particular big client, a certain person's endorsement, a lucky break, or any other common excuse not to start.)

Ideas are just a multiplier of execution

It's so funny when I hear people being so protective of ideas (especially people who want me to sign a non-disclosure agreement before they tell me about the simplest ideas).

To me, ideas are worth nothing unless they are executed. They are just a multiplier. Execution is worth millions.

Explanation:

> **Awful idea = -1**
> **Weak idea = 1**
> **So-so idea = 5**
> **Good idea = 10**
> **Great idea = 15**
> **Brilliant idea = 20**
>
> **No execution = $1**
> **Weak execution = $1,000**
> **So-so execution = $10,000**
> **Good execution = $100,000**
> **Great execution = $1,000,000**
> **Brilliant execution = $10,000,000**

To make a business, you need to multiply the two components. The most brilliant idea, with no execution, is worth $20. The most brilliant idea takes great execution to be worth $200,000,000.

That's why I don't want to hear people's ideas. I'm not interested until I see their execution.

Formalities play on fear. Bravely refuse.

A year after starting CD Baby, when it was going pretty well, I got a call from a friend who was setting up his own similar web-based business. He said, "Do you have any advice about how to do our 'Terms and Conditions' and 'Privacy Policy' on the website? Which lawyer did you use for that?"

I said, "Huh? I don't have any of that legalese stuff. I've never hired a lawyer."

Shocked, he said, "That's crazy! What if some kid buys a CD from you, then kills himself? What if you get sued over that?"

I said, "Then no stupid footnote legalese would protect me anyway, so I'll worry about it if it happens."

Do you passionately love the "Terms & Conditions" and "Privacy Policy" pages on other websites? Have you even read them? If not, then why would you go putting that garbage on your website?

After CD Baby grew to fifty employees, all the business-to-business service companies started pitching me on how I needed an official employee review plan, sensitivity training, Terms and Conditions postings, and all this corporate crap. I got such joy out of saying no to all of it.

Never forget that there are thousands of businesses, like

Jim's Fish Bait Shop in a shack on a beach somewhere, that are doing just fine without corporate formalities.

As your business grows, don't let the leeches sucker you into all that stuff they pretend you need. They'll play on your fears, saying that you need this stuff to protect yourself against lawsuits. They'll scare you with horrible worst-case scenarios. But those are just sales tactics. You don't need any of it.

The strength of many little customers

Many small entrepreneurs think, "If we can just land Apple, Google, or the government as a client, we'll be all set!"

Software companies often do this. They hope to make some technology that a huge company will want to build into every product or install at every employee's desk.

But this approach has many problems:

▶ You have to custom-tailor your product to please a very few specific people.

▶ Those people might change their minds or leave the company.

▶ Whom are you really working for? Are you self-employed or is this client your boss?

▶ If you do land the big client, that organization will practically own you.

▶ By trying so hard to please the big client, you will lose touch with what the rest of the world wants.

Instead, imagine that you have designed your business to have *no* big clients, just lots of little clients.

▶ You don't need to change what you do to please one client; you need to please only the majority (or yourself).

▶ If one client needs to leave, it's OK; you can sincerely wish her well.

▶ Because no one client can demand that you do what he says, you are your own boss (as long as you keep your clients happy in general).

▶ You hear hundreds of people's opinions and stay in touch with what the majority of your clients want.

So much of the music business is actually the star business—people hoping to catch the coattails of a redundant megastar. But I wanted nothing to do with that, for these same reasons.

When you build your business on serving thousands of customers, not dozens, you don't have to worry about any one customer leaving or making special demands. If most of your customers love what you do, but one doesn't, you can just say good-bye and wish him the best, with no hard feelings.

Proudly exclude people

You know you can't please everyone, right?

But notice that most businesses are trying to be everything to everybody. And they wonder why they can't get people's attention!

You need to confidently exclude people, and proudly say what you're not. By doing so, you will win the hearts of the people you want.

The Hotel Café, a folk- and rock-music venue in Los Angeles, is a no-talking club. Big signs read, NO TALKING DURING PERFORMANCES! Performers are encouraged to stop the show if someone is talking, and let the person know that he can go to any other club in town to talk over the music. This is the one place in L.A. where you can sit and really listen to the music, which, of course, makes it the most popular music venue in town.

When CD Baby got popular, I'd get calls from record labels wanting to feature their newest, hottest acts on our site.

I'd say, "Nope. They're not allowed here."

The record label guys would say, "Huh? What do you mean not allowed? You're a record store! We're a record label."

I'd say, "You can sell anywhere else. This is a place for independents only: musicians who chose not to sign their rights over to a corporation. To make sure these musicians get the maximum exposure they deserve, no major-label acts are allowed."

It's a big world. You can loudly leave out 99 percent of it.

Have the confidence to know that when your target 1 percent hears you excluding the other 99 percent, the people in that 1 percent will come to you because you've shown how much you value them.

Why no advertising?

I got a call from an advertising salesman saying he'd like to run banner ads at the top and bottom of cdbaby.com.

I said, "No way. Out of the question. That would be like putting a Coke machine in a monastery. I'm not doing this to make money."

He said, "But you're a business. What do you mean you're not trying to make money?"

I said, "I'm just trying to help musicians. CD Baby has to charge money to sustain itself, but the money's not the point. I don't do anything for the money."

This goes back to the utopian perfect-world ideal of why we're doing what we're doing in the first place. In a perfect world, would your website be covered with advertising? When you've asked your customers what would improve your service, has anyone said, "Please fill your website with more advertising"?

Nope. So don't do it.

This is just one of many options

I used to take voice lessons from a great teacher named Warren Senders. For each lesson, I'd bring in one song I was trying to improve. First, I'd sing it for him as written.

Then he'd say, "OK, now do it up an octave."

"Uh . . . up an octave? But I can't sing that high!"

"I don't care! Do it anyway! Go! One, two, three, four."

I'd sing the whole song again, in screeching, squeaking falsetto, sounding like an undead cartoon mouse. But by the second half of the song, it was almost charming.

Then he'd say, "OK, now do it down an octave."

"Down an octave? But I don't think I can!"

"Doesn't matter! Go! One, two, three, four."

I sounded like a garbage disposal or lawn mower, but he made me sing the whole song that way.

Then he'd make me sing it twice as fast. Then twice as slow. Then like Bob Dylan. Then like Tom Waits. Then he'd tell me to sing it like it's 4 a.m. and a friend woke me up. And then he'd give me many other scenarios.

After all of this, he'd say, "Now, how did that song go again?" It was the clearest proof that what I thought was "the" way the song went was really just one of an infinite number of options.

I'm taking an entrepreneurship class now. I've never studied business before.

We analyzed a business plan for a mail-order pantyhose company. Like all business plans, it proposed only one idea. After reading the whole thing, I felt like saying things my old voice teacher would have said:

▶ "OK, make a plan that requires only $1,000. Go!"

▶ "Now make a plan for ten times as many customers. Go!"

▶ "Now do it without a website. Go!"

▶ "Now make all your initial assumptions wrong, and have it work anyway. Go!"

▶ "Now show how you would franchise it. Go!"

You can't pretend there's only one way to do it. Your first idea is just one of many options. No business goes as planned, so make ten radically different plans.

Same thing with your current path in life:

▶ Now you're living in New York City, obsessed with success. Go!

▶ Now you're a free spirit, backpacking around Thailand. Go!

▶ Now you're a confident extrovert and everyone loves you. Go!

▶ Now you're married and your kids are your life. Go!

▶ Now you spend a few years in relative seclusion, reading and walking. Go!

You don't need a plan or a vision

Do you have a big visionary master plan for how the world will work in twenty years? Do you have massive ambitions to revolutionize your industry?

Don't feel bad if you don't. I never did.

A year and a half after starting CD Baby, it was just me and John, my first employee, running it out of my house. One night, I decided I should think more about the long-term future of this thing. I sat with my diary for a few hours of introspection. Afterward, I wrote John an e-mail that went like this:

"I think there's a chance that this thing might be huge one day, so we better start preparing for that now. I mean someday, we might have ONE THOUSAND artists on CD Baby. We might need a third employee! That would mean we'd need three computers here in the office, which would mean we'd need to figure out how to network them together. We might even need to start moving CDs into the garage, since eventually they might fill up the living room. Yes, I know it sounds grandiose, but I think things are headed that way."

Years later, after I had a hundred thousand artists and eighty-five employees, John would often get a good laugh out of this e-mail I sent him in 1999.

Journalists would ask, "What's your long-term goal for CD Baby?"

I'd say, "I don't have one. I surpassed my goals long ago. I'm just trying to help musicians with whatever they need today."

So please don't think you need a huge vision. Just stay focused on helping people today.

"I miss the mob."

I was in Las Vegas for a conference, taking a taxi from the airport to the hotel. I asked the driver, "How long have you lived here?"

He said, "Twenty-seven years."

"Wow! A lot has changed since then, huh?"

"Yeah. I miss the mob."

"Huh? Really? What do you mean?"

"When the mafia ran this town, it was fun. There were only two numbers that mattered: how much was coming in, and how much was going out. As long as there was more in than out, everyone was happy. But then the whole town was bought up by these damn corporations full of MBA weasels micromanaging, trying to maximize the profit from every square foot of floor space. Now the place that used to put ketchup on my hot dog tells me it'll be an extra twenty-five cents for ketchup! It sucked all the fun out of this town! Yeah, I miss the mob." (Sure, we could bring up other issues with the mob, but let's just leave it as a metaphor and a lesson.)

I told this story a lot at CD Baby. Sometimes MBA types would ask me, "What's your growth rate? What's your retained earnings rate as a percentage of gross? What are your projections?"

I'd just say, "I have no idea. I don't even know what some of that means. I started this as a hobby to help my friends, and that's the only reason it exists. There's money in the bank and I'm doing fine, so no worries."

They'd tell me that if I analyzed the business better, I could maximize profitability. Then I'd tell them about the taxi driver in Vegas.

Never forget why you're really doing what you're doing. Are you helping people? Are they happy? Are you happy? Are you profitable? Isn't that enough?

How do you grade yourself?

In New York City, there are dozens of buildings that say TRUMP on them. As I was driving about an hour into the rural country-side, I even saw a Donald J. Trump park. It made me wonder if he grades himself according to how many valuable properties bear his name. Plenty of real estate tycoons have made billions without putting their names on everything, but maybe that's his measure.

We all grade ourselves by different measures:

- For some people, it's as simple as how much money they make. When their net worth is going up, they know they're doing well.

- For others, it's how much money they give.

- For some, it's how many people's lives they can influence for the better.

- For others, it's how deeply they can influence just a few people's lives.

For me, it's how many useful things I create, whether songs, companies, articles, websites, or anything else. If I create something that's not useful to others, it doesn't count. But I'm also not interested in doing something useful unless it needs my creative input.

How do you grade yourself?

It's important to know in advance, to make sure you're staying focused on what's honestly important to you, instead of doing what others think you should.

Care about your customers more than about yourself

At a conference in Los Angeles, someone in the audience asked me, "What if every musician just set up their own store on their own website? Since that'd be the death of CD Baby, how do you plan to stop that?"

I said, "Honestly, I don't care about CD Baby. I only care about the musicians. If someday, musicians don't need CD Baby anymore, that's great! I'll just shut it down and get back to making music."

He was shocked. He had never heard a business owner say he didn't care about the survival of his company.

To me, it was just common sense. Of course you should care about your customers more than you care about yourself! Isn't that Rule No. 1 of providing a good service? It's all about them, not about you.

But even well-meaning companies accidentally get trapped in survival mode. A business is started to solve a problem. But if the problem were truly solved, that business would no longer be needed! So the business accidentally or unconsciously keeps the problem around so that they can keep solving it for a fee. (I don't want to pick on anyone's favorite pharmaceutical company or online productivity subscription tools, so let's just say that any business that's in business to sell you a cure is motivated not to focus on prevention.)

It's kind of like the grand tales in which the hero needs to be prepared to die to save the day. Your company should be willing to die for your customers.

That's the Tao of business: Care about your customers more than about yourself, and you'll do well.

Act like you don't need the money

Banks love to lend money to those who don't need it. Record labels love to sign musicians who don't need their help. People fall in love with people who won't give them the time of day. It's a strange law of human behavior. It's pretty universal.

If you set up your business like you don't need the money, people are happier to pay you. When someone's doing something for the money, people can sense it, like they sense a desperate lover. It's a turnoff. When someone's doing something for love, being generous instead of stingy, trusting instead of fearful, it triggers this law: We want to give to those who give.

It's another Tao of business: Set up your business like you don't need the money, and it'll likely come your way.

Don't punish everyone for one person's mistake

The little diner near me has these big warning signs posted everywhere:

**WE RESERVE THE RIGHT TO REFUSE SERVICE
TO ANYONE FOR ANY REASON**

**ALL ORDERS ARE FINAL!
ABSOLUTELY NO REFUNDS!**

NO SHOES, NO SHIRT, NO SERVICE

NO CELL PHONES. NO PHOTOS. NO VIDEOS.

**NO LOITERING!
RESTROOM FOR CUSTOMERS ONLY!**

**ALL VIOLATORS WILL BE PROSECUTED
TO THE FULLEST EXTENT OF THE LAW**

That poor business owner needs a hug. Every time someone upsets him, he punishes all his future customers forever.

When I was six, I attended a strict little school in Abingdon, England. Early in the year, someone spilled grape juice. So grape juice was banned for the rest of the year. Later, someone spilled orange juice, so orange juice was banned for the rest of the year. Eventually we were allowed nothing but water.

Several years ago, one guy tried to light his shoes on fire on a plane. Now, and for all future time, millions of people a day have to queue up to take their shoes off at the airport—because of that one dumb moment.

As a business owner, when you get screwed over by someone, you might be tempted to make a big grand policy that you think will prevent your ever getting screwed over again: One employee can't focus and spends his time surfing the Web. Instead of just firing or reassigning that person to more challenging work, the company installs an expensive content-approving firewall so that nobody can go to unapproved sites ever again.

It's important to resist that simplistic, angry, reactionary urge to punish everyone, and step back to look at the big picture. In the moment, you're angry, focusing only on that one awful person who did you wrong. Your thinking is clouded. You start believing everyone is awful and the whole world is against you. This is a horrible time to make a new policy.

When one customer wrongs you, remember the hundred thousand who did not. You're lucky to own your own business. Life is good. You can't prevent bad things from happening. Learn to shrug. Resist the urge to punish everyone for one person's mistake.

A real person, a lot like you

My friend Sara has run a small online business out of her living room for twelve years. It's her whole life. She takes it very, very personally.

Recently, one of her clients sent her a ten-page scathing e-mail, chopping her down, calling her a scam artist and issuing other vicious personal insults, saying she was going to sue Sara for everything she's worth as retribution for the client's mishandled account.

Devastated, Sara turned off her computer and cried. She shut off the phones and closed up shop for the day. She spent the whole weekend in bed wondering if she should just give up, thinking maybe every insult in this client's letter is true and she's actually no good at what she does, even after twelve years.

On Sunday, she spent about five hours—most of the day— carefully addressing every point in this ten-page e-mail; then she went through the client's website, learning everything about her, and offered all kinds of advice, suggestions, and connections. Sara refunded the client's money, plus an additional $50, with deep apologies for ever having upset someone she was honestly trying to help.

The next day, she called the client to try to talk through the situation with her. The client cheerfully took her call and said, "Oh, don't worry about it! I wasn't actually that upset. I was just in a bad mood, and didn't think anyone would read my e-mail anyway."

My friend Valerie was using an online dating service. She was halfhearted about it. She wanted a magic perfect man to sweep her off her feet through divine serendipity.

We were at her computer when I asked her how it was going. She logged in to her account and showed me her in-box. There were eight new messages, each one well written, saying what the man liked about her profile, how they have a mutual interest in hiking, or that he also speaks German, and asking her if she's also been to Berlin, or has hiked in New Zealand.

I felt for those guys, each one pouring out his heart, projecting his hopes onto Valerie, hoping she'd reply with equal enthusiasm, hoping she might be the one who would finally see and appreciate him.

She said, "Ugh. Losers. I get, like, ten of these a day." Then she deleted all of them, without replying.

When we yell at our car or our coffee machine, it's fine because they're just mechanical appliances. So when we yell at a website or a company, using our computer or our phone, we forget that it's not an appliance but a person that's affected.

It's dehumanizing to have thousands of people passing through our computer screens, so we do things we'd never do if those people were sitting next to us. It's too overwhelming to remember that at the end of every computer is a real person, a lot like you, whose birthday was last week, who has three best friends but nobody to spoon at night, and who is personally affected by what you say.

Even if you remember it right now, will you remember it next time you're overwhelmed, or perhaps never forget it again?

You should feel pain when you're unclear

E-mail blasts are the best training for being clear.

CD Baby had about two million customers.

When writing an e-mail to everyone, if I wasn't perfectly clear, I'd get twenty thousand confused replies, which would take my staff all week to reply to, costing me at least $5,000 plus lost morale. Even if I was very clear but took more than a few sentences to explain something, I'd get thousands of replies from people who never read past the first few sentences.

Writing that e-mail to customers—carefully eliminating every unnecessary word, and reshaping every sentence to make sure it could not be misunderstood—would take me all day. One unclear sentence? Immediate $5,000 penalty. Ouch.

Unfortunately, people writing websites don't get this kind of feedback. Instead, if they're not clear, they just get silence—lots of hits but no action.

I see new websites trying to look impressive, filled with hundreds of puffy, unnecessary sentences. I feel bad that the people behind those sites haven't felt the pain of trying to e-mail that text to thousands of people, to directly see how misunderstood or ignored it is.

The most successful e-mail I ever wrote

When you make a business, you're making a little world where you control the laws. It doesn't matter how things are done everywhere else. In your little world, you can make it like it should be.

When I first built CD Baby, every order resulted in an automated e-mail that let the customer know when the CD was actually shipped. At first this note was just the normal "Your order has shipped today. Please let us know if it doesn't arrive. Thank you for your business."

After a few months, that felt really incongruent with my mission to make people smile. I knew I could do better. So I took twenty minutes and wrote this goofy little thing:

> Your CD has been gently taken from our CD Baby shelves with sterilized contamination-free gloves and placed onto a satin pillow.
>
> A team of 50 employees inspected your CD and polished it to make sure it was in the best possible condition before mailing.
>
> Our packing specialist from Japan lit a candle and a hush fell over the crowd as he put your CD into the finest gold-lined box that money can buy.
>
> We all had a wonderful celebration afterwards and the whole party marched down the street to the post office where the entire town of Portland waved "Bon Voyage!" to your package,

> on its way to you, in our private CD Baby jet on this day, Friday,
> June 6th.
>
> I hope you had a wonderful time shopping at CD Baby. We
> sure did. Your picture is on our wall as "Customer of the Year."
> We're all exhausted but can't wait for you to come back
> to CDBABY.COM!!

That one silly e-mail, sent out with every order, has been so loved that if you search Google for "private CD Baby jet," you'll get almost twenty thousand results. Each one is somebody who got the e-mail and loved it enough to post it on his website and tell all his friends. That one goofy e-mail created thousands of new customers.

When you're thinking of how to make your business bigger, it's tempting to try to think all the big thoughts and come up with world-changing massive-action plans. But please know that it's often the tiny details that really thrill people enough to make them tell all their friends about you.

Little things make all the difference

If you find even the smallest way to make people smile, they'll remember you more for that smile than for all your other fancy business-model stuff.

Here are some things that made a huge difference on the CD Baby website:

Because we shipped FedEx at 5 p.m. each day, customers would often call and ask, "What time is it there? Do I still have time to get it sent today?" So I added two little lines of programming code that counted how many hours and minutes remained until 5 p.m. and then showed the result by the shipping options. "You have 5 hours, 18 minutes until our next FedEx shipment." Customers *loved* this!

We answered our phone within two rings, always—7 a.m. to 10 p.m., seven days a week. Phones were everywhere, so even if the customer service rep was busy, someone in the warehouse could pick up. All anyone had to do was say, "CD Baby!" Customers *loved* this! Someone actually picking up the phone at a company is so rare that musicians would often tell me later at conferences that it was the main reason they decided to go with CD Baby—they could always talk to a real person immediately. All employees knew that as long as we weren't completely swamped, they should take a minute and get to know the caller a bit. Ask about her music. Ask how it's going. Yes, it would lead to twenty-minute conversations sometimes, but those people became lifelong fans.

Every outgoing e-mail has a "From:" name, right? Why not use that to make people smile, too? With one line of code, I made it so that every outgoing e-mail customized the "From:" field to be "CD Baby loves [first name]." So if the customer's name was Susan, every e-mail she got from us would say it was from "CD Baby loves Susan." Customers *loved* this!

Sometimes, after we had done the forty-five minutes of work to add a new album to the store, the musician would change his mind and ask us to do it over again with a different album cover or different audio clips. I wanted to say yes but let him know that this was really hard to do, so I made a policy that made us both smile: "We'll do anything for a pizza." If you needed a big special favor, we'd give you the number of our local pizza delivery place. If you bought us a pizza, we'd do any favor you wanted. When we'd tell people about this on the phone, they'd often laugh, not believing we were serious. But we'd get a pizza every few weeks. I'd often hear from musicians later that this was the moment they fell in love with us.

At the end of each order, the last page of the website would ask, "Where did you hear of this artist? We'll pass them any message you write here." Customers would often take the time to write things like, "Heard your song on WBEZ radio last night." "Searched Yahoo!" "Found it here." "I'd love to have you play at our school!" The musicians absolutely loved getting this information, and it always led to the customer and musician getting in touch directly. This is something that big stores like Amazon would never do.

Also at the end of each order, there was a box that would ask, "Any special requests?" One time, someone said, "I'd love some cinnamon gum." Since one of the guys in the warehouse was going to the store anyway, he picked up some cinnamon gum and included it in the package. One time, someone said, "If you could include a small, rubber squid, I would appreciate it. If this is unobtainable, a real squid would do." Just by chance, a customer from Korea had sent us a packaged filet of squid. So the shipping guys included it in the box with the other customer's CDs. See the customer tell the story himself in this great video: http://sivers.org/squid.

Even if you want to be big someday, remember that you never need to act like a big boring company. Over ten years, it seemed like every time someone raved about how much he loved CD Baby, it was because of one of these little fun human touches.

It's OK to be casual

My hiring policy was ridiculous. Because I was "too busy to bother," I'd just ask my current employees if they had any friends who needed work. Someone always did, so I'd say, "Tell them to start tomorrow morning. Ten dollars an hour. Show them what to do." And that was that.

The thought was that it's almost impossible to tell what someone's going to be like on the job until he's actually on the job for a few weeks. So I'd hire lightly and fire lightly. Luckily we didn't need to fire that often. Maybe the fact that the new hires were friends of friends helped with the trust part.

To be fair, this was a mail-order CD store, so most of my employees were in the warehouse. But I also took this same casual approach when I needed an important high-tech systems administrator: "Anyone have a friend who's good with Linux? Yeah? Is he cool? OK, tell him to start tomorrow."

The first time I did that I found Ryan. The second time, I found Jason. Both guys are amazing and are key people at CD Baby to this day.

Don't try to impress an invisible jury of MBA professors. It's OK to be casual.

Naive quitting

My first real job was as the librarian at Warner/Chappell Music. I loved it. I was twenty years old, and I had just graduated from Berklee College of Music, in Boston, and moved to New York City. I took the job very seriously and learned a lot.

After two and a half years, though, I decided to quit to be a full-time musician. (Partially because I was too happy there! I was scared that if I didn't force myself to quit, I'd never leave. I was too comfortable.)

Since I had never quit a job before and didn't know how, I did what seemed to be the respectful and considerate thing to do: I found and trained my replacement. (It wasn't my boss's fault I wanted to quit, so why should I make it his problem? If I want to quit, it's my problem.) I called on my old friend Nikki, who I knew would be perfect, and offered her my job at my current salary. She came with me to the office for a week while I trained her in every aspect of the job. Once she had it mastered, I went into my boss's office on a Friday afternoon and said, "I need to quit now, but I've already trained my replacement. She's great. She'll take over for me starting Monday."

My boss just looked a little stunned, then said, "Uh. Well. OK. We'll miss you. Tell her to see HR about the paperwork." And that was that.

Ten years later, I was running CD Baby, and for the first time, an employee told me he needed to quit.

I said, "Drag. Well. OK. I wish you the best! Who's your replacement?"

He looked confused.

I said, "Have you found and trained a replacement yet?"

He looked a little stunned, then said, "No . . . . I think that's your job."

Now I was stunned. I asked a few friends and found out he was right. People can just quit a job without finding and training their replacements. I had no idea. All these years, I just assumed what I had done was normal.

There's a benefit to being naive about the norms of the world—deciding from scratch what seems like the right thing to do, instead of just doing what others do.

Prepare to double

CD Baby doubled in size every year for the first six years. Both customers and profit, almost exactly 100 percent growth each year. It was spooky.

Because the business needed a warehouse for the CDs, I always had to buy more shelving. Each time I did, I'd buy twice as much as I had before. It always filled up fast, even when it got warehouse-sized. When I had filled a 5,000-square-foot warehouse, I rented 10,000 square feet. When I filled up 10,000 square feet, I rented 20,000 square feet. Even that filled up fast.

But no matter what business you're in, it's good to prepare for what would happen if business doubled. Have ten clients now? How would it look if you had twenty at once? Serving eighty customers for lunch each day? What would happen if 160 showed up?

Notice that "more of the same" is never the answer. You'd have to do things in a new way to handle twice as much business. Processes would have to be streamlined.

Never be the typical tragic small business that gets frazzled and freaked out when business is doing well. It sends a repulsive "I can't handle this!" message to everyone. Instead, if your internal processes are always designed to handle twice your existing load, it sends an attractive "come on in, we've got plenty of room" message.

It's about being, not having

Being a singer:

Since I was fourteen, I was determined to be a great singer. But my pitch was bad, my tone was bad, and everyone said I was just not a singer.

For eleven years, from the ages of fourteen to twenty-five, I took voice lessons, and practiced at least an hour a day. I was always the lead singer of my band, doing a few shows a week, getting as much real-world experience as possible. The whole time, people kept telling me I was just not a singer—that I should give it up and find a real singer.

When I was twenty-five, I recorded my first album. When I gave it to someone who was a real mentor to me, he gave it a focused listen and then said, "Derek, you're just not a singer. You really need to stop trying. Admit you're a songwriter, and find a real singer." But I bounced away from that meeting unfazed. I knew I just had more work to do.

At twenty-eight, I started noticing that my voice was getting good! I recorded a few new songs, and for the first time, I really liked the vocals!

At twenty-nine, I had done it. After fifteen years of practice, and about a thousand live shows, I was finally a very good singer, at least by my own standards. (Someone who heard me for the first time then said, "Singing is a gift you're either born with or you're not. You're lucky. You were born with it!")

Point is: It's not that I wanted to get it done and have good vocals. It's that I wanted to be a great singer.

Being a producer:

I wanted to record my album myself, to learn recording-studio engineering and production, because I thought that would be a really rewarding and empowering thing to know how to do—like building your own house.

Friends and mentors said that was ridiculous, that I should just hire a great engineer, producer, and studio. Doing everything myself might take years, whereas I could have it all done in a few weeks if I just hired someone good.

I took the few years to learn it myself, and it was one of the most rewarding experiences of my life. For the next few years, I did all the production and engineering on a few friends' albums, too. Now it's something I know how to do, and it feels great.

Being a programmer:

When I started CD Baby, I knew only some basic HTML, no programming. But as the site grew, basic HTML wouldn't do it anymore. My tech friends told me I had to make a server-side database-driven automated system.

Since I couldn't afford to hire a programmer, that meant I had to learn it myself. I went to the bookstore and got a book on PHP and MySQL programming. It was the slow road, but I loved it! As with being in the recording studio again, it was wonderful to learn how to make the technology do what I wanted and not be a mystery. And it was nice to be self-sufficient.

As the company grew, everyone was surprised that I still did all the programming myself. But for an Internet business, outsourcing the programming would be like a band outsourcing the songwriting! This wasn't just my business—this was my creation. This wasn't like mowing lawns—this was like writing songs.

In the last few years, my employees got furious that new features were not being added as fast as they wanted, because I still insisted on doing all the programming myself. They said we were losing millions of dollars in business because we didn't have certain features. But that was OK with me. I loved the process. I was happy.

Being, not having:

When you want to learn how to do something yourself, most people won't understand. They'll assume the only reason we do anything is to get it done, and doing it yourself is not the most efficient way.

But that's forgetting about the joy of learning and doing. Yes, it may take longer. Yes, it may be inefficient. Yes, it may even cost you millions of dollars in lost opportunities because your business is growing slower because you're insisting on doing something yourself. But the whole point of doing anything is because it makes you happy! That's it!

You might get bigger faster and make millions if you outsource everything to the experts. But what's the point of getting bigger and making millions? To be happy, right?

In the end, it's about what you want to be, not what you want to have. To have something (a finished recording, a business, or millions of dollars) is the means, not the end. To be something (a good singer, a skilled entrepreneur, or just plain happy) is the real point.

When you sign up to run a marathon, you don't want a taxi to take you to the finish line.

The day Steve Jobs dissed me in a keynote

In May 2003, Apple invited me to their headquarters to discuss getting CD Baby's catalog into the iTunes Music Store. iTunes had just launched two weeks before, with only some music from the major labels. Many of us in the music biz—especially those who had seen companies like eMusic use this exact same model for years without much success—were not sure this idea was going to work.

I flew to Cupertino, California, thinking I'd be meeting with one of Apple's marketing or tech people. When I arrived, I found out that about a hundred people from small record labels and distributors had also been invited.

We all went into a little presentation room, not knowing what to expect. Then out came Steve Jobs. Whoa! Wow. He was in full persuasive presentation mode—trying to convince all of us to give Apple our entire catalog of music, talking about iTunes' success so far, and all the reasons we should work with Apple. He made a point of saying, "We want the iTunes Music Store to have every piece of music ever recorded. Even if it's discontinued or not selling much, we want it all."

This was huge to me, because until 2003, independent musicians were always denied access to the big outlets. For Apple to sell all music, not just music from artists who had signed their rights away to a corporation—this was amazing!

Then the Apple guys showed us the software we'd all have to use to send them each album. It required us to put the audio CD into a Mac CD-ROM drive; type in all of the album info, the song titles, and the artist's bio; click Encode for it to rip; and click Upload when done.

I raised my hand and asked if it was required that we use their software. They said yes. I asked again, saying we had more than a hundred thousand albums, already ripped as lossless WAV files, with all of the info carefully entered by the artists themselves, ready to send to Apple's servers with their exact specifications.

The Apple guys said, "Sorry, you need to use this software; there is no other way."

Ugh. That meant we'd have to pull each one of those CDs off of the shelf again, stick it in a Mac, and cut and paste every song title into that Mac software. But so be it. If that's what Apple needed, OK.

They said they'd be ready for us to start uploading in the next couple of weeks.

I flew home that night, posted my meeting notes on my website, e-mailed all of my clients to announce the news, and went to sleep.

When I woke, I had furious e-mails and voice mails from my contact at Apple: "What the hell are you doing? That meeting was confidential! Take those notes off your site immediately! Our legal department is furious!"

There had been no mention of confidentiality at the meeting and no agreement to sign. But I removed my notes from my site immediately, to be nice. All was well, or so I thought.

Apple e-mailed us the iTunes Music Store contract. We immediately signed it and returned it the same day. I started building the system to deliver everyone's music to iTunes.

I decided we'd have to charge $40 for this service to cover our bandwidth and the payroll costs of pulling each CD out of the warehouse, entering all the info, digitizing and uploading the music, and putting the CD back in the warehouse.

Five thousand musicians signed up in advance, each paying $40. That $200,000 helped pay for the extra equipment and people needed to make this happen.

Within two weeks, we got contacted by Rhapsody, Yahoo! Music, Napster, eMusic, and more, each saying they wanted our entire catalog. Yes! Awesome!

Maybe you can't appreciate this now, but the summer of 2003 was the biggest turning point that independent music has ever had. Until that point, almost no big business would sell independent music. With iTunes saying they wanted everything, and then their competitors needing to keep up, we were in! Since the summer of 2003, all musicians everywhere have been able to sell all their music in almost every outlet online. Do you realize how amazing that is?

But there was one problem. iTunes wasn't getting back to us. Yahoo!, Rhapsody, Napster, and the rest were all up and running. But iTunes wasn't returning our signed contract. Was it because I had posted my meeting notes? Had I pissed off Steve

Jobs? Nobody at Apple would say anything. It had been months. My musicians were getting impatient and angry.

I gave optimistic apologies, but I was starting to get worried, too.

A month later, Steve Jobs did a special worldwide simulcast keynote speech about iTunes. People had been criticizing iTunes for having less music than the competition. They had 400,000 songs, while Rhapsody and Napster had more than 2 million songs. (More than 500,000 of those were from CD Baby.)

Four minutes in, he said something that made my pounding heart sink to my burning stomach:

"This number could have easily been much higher, if we wanted to let in every song. But we realize record companies do a great service. They edit! Did you know that if you and I record a song, for $40 we can pay a few of the services to get it on their site, through some intermediaries? We can be on Rhapsody and all these other guys for $40? Well, we don't want to let that stuff on our site! So we've had to edit it. And these are 400,000 quality songs."

Whoa! Wow. Steve Jobs had just dissed me hard! I was the only one charging $40. That was me he was referring to!

Shit. OK. That's that. Steve changed his mind. No independents on iTunes. You heard the man.

I hated the position this put me in. Ever since I started my company in 1998, I had been offering excellent service. I could make promises and keep them because I was in full control. Now, for the first time, I had promised something that was out of my control.

So it was time to do the right thing, no matter how much it hurt. I decided to refund everybody's $40, with my deepest apologies. With five thousand musicians signed up, that meant I was refunding $200,000.

Since we couldn't promise anything, I couldn't charge money in good conscience. I removed all mention of iTunes from my site. I removed the $40 cost. I decided to make digital distribution a free service from that point on. I changed the language to say we couldn't promise anything. I e-mailed everyone to let them know what had happened.

The very next day, I got our signed contract back from Apple, along with upload instructions. Unbelievable. I asked, "Why now?" but got no answer. Whatever. Fucking Apple.

We started encoding and uploading immediately. I quietly added iTunes back to the list of companies on our site.

But I never again promised a customer that I could do something that was beyond my full control.

My $3.3 million mistake

Starting when I was a teenager, my dad would occasionally send me things to sign for the family business. I didn't understand the complexities of it, and didn't need to, so I'd just sign without question.

Four years before I started CD Baby, as I was recording my first album, I needed to borrow $20,000 to buy studio equipment. My dad said, "Instead of my lending you money, start a corporation. Then the family business can buy shares in your corporation."

So I did. Because my band was called Hit Me, I called the company Hit Media Inc. My dad's company bought some shares, and that helped me finish my album, and I continued to run my record studio at a profit.

Four years later, I was living in Woodstock, New York, and started this little hobby called CD Baby.

The first time I got a check addressed to "CD Baby," I brought it down to the bank and told the teller, "I need to set this up as a new business, so let's open a new business account."

She said, "Oh you don't need to do that. You can just make it an alias on your Hit Media account." (At that time, Hit Media was a recording studio and booking agency.) It seemed a little strange because CD Baby was definitely a new business, but it saved ten minutes and $100, so I said OK.

Four years later, CD Baby was doing really well: a few million dollars in sales, half a million dollars in net profits. I paid my dad back the $20,000 I had borrowed.

I called up my accountant in January. "OK. I got all the Quicken books balanced. Should we file early this year?"

He said, "Oh, you don't need to file. CD Baby is just a line item on your dad's company's tax return."

I said, "Uh . . . what?"

"You didn't know that your dad's company owns ninety percent of CD Baby?"

"Uh . . . what?"

"You should talk to your dad."

Yes, it turns out that when I borrowed the $20,000 eight years earlier, I didn't realize that I got the $20,000 by selling 90 percent of Hit Media Inc. to my dad's company. Then because the bank teller advised me to make CD Baby an alias of Hit Media, that meant my dad's company owned 90 percent of CD Baby as well.

FFFFffff . . . SSSSssss . . . RRRRrrrr . . . Oh, what a horrible sinking feeling. What I thought was my company all these years was not actually my company. I owned only 10 percent.

I couldn't be mad at my dad. He was doing me a favor back then and thought I knew what I was signing. Nobody thought my little hobby was going to turn into a multimillion-dollar business. It was my fault for not reading what I signed. My fault for letting a bank teller's quick advice make that major decision for my business structure.

What made it even worse is that I couldn't just buy the business back for the original $20,000. The IRS wouldn't allow that. The only way was to pay full market value, as determined by an outside valuation company.

In the end, I had to pay $3.3 million to buy back that 90 percent of my company.

Delegate or die:
The self-employment trap

Most self-employed people get caught in the delegation trap.

You're so busy, doing everything yourself. You know you need help, but to find and train someone would take more time than you have. So you keep working harder, until you break.

Here's my little tale of how I broke into the delegation mind-set:

In 2001, CD Baby was three years old. I had eight employees, but I was still doing "everything else" myself, working 7 a.m. to 10 p.m., seven days a week. Everything still went through me.

Every five minutes, my employees had a question for me:

"Derek, some guy wants to change the album art after it's already live on the site. What do I tell him?"

"Derek, can we accept wire transfer as a form of payment?"

"Derek, someone placed two orders today, and wants to know if we can ship them together as one, but refund him the shipping cost savings."

It was hard to get anything done while answering questions all day. I felt like I might as well just show up to work and sit on a chair in the hallway, just answering employees' questions full-time.

I hit my breaking point. I stopped going to the office and

shut off my phone. Then I realized I was running from my problems instead of solving them. I had to fix this, or I'd be ruined.

After a long night of thinking and writing, I got myself into the delegation mind-set. I had to make myself unnecessary to the running of my company.

The next day, as soon as I walked in the door, someone said, "Derek, someone whose CDs we received yesterday has now changed his mind and wants his CDs shipped back. We've already done the work, but he's asking if we can refund his setup fee since he was never live on the site."

This time, instead of just answering the question, I called everyone together for a minute. I repeated the situation and the question. I answered the question, but more important, I explained the thought process and philosophy behind my answer.

"Yes, refund his money in full. We'll take a little loss. It's important to always do whatever would make the customer happiest, as long as it's not outrageous. A little gesture like this goes a long way toward him telling his friends we're a great company. Everyone always remember that helping musicians is our first goal, and profit is second. You have my full permission to use that guideline to make these decisions yourself in the future. Do what makes the musicians happiest. Make sure everyone who deals with us leaves with a smile."

I asked around to make sure everyone understood the answer. I asked one person to start a manual, and write down the answer to this one situation, along with the philosophy behind it. Then everyone went back to work.

Ten minutes later, a new question. Same process:

1. Gather everybody around.

2. Answer the question and explain the philosophy.

3. Make sure everyone understands the thought process.

4. Ask one person to write it in the manual.

5. Let everybody know they can decide this without me next time.

After two months of this, there were no more questions.

Then I showed someone how to do the last of the stuff that was still my job. As part of learning it, he had to document it in the manual, and then show it to someone else, too. (Learn by teaching.)

Now I was totally unnecessary. I started working at home, not going into the office at all.

I had even taught the employees my thought process and philosophy about hiring new people. So our two newest employees were found, interviewed, hired, and trained by other employees. They used that manual to make sure all new employees understood the philosophy and history of CD Baby, and knew how to make decisions for themselves.

I'd call in once a week to make sure everything was OK. It was. No one had any questions for me.

Because my team was running the business, I was free to actually improve the business! I moved to California, just to make it clear that the running of things was up to the employees. I was still working twelve-hour days, but now I was spending all my time on improvements, optimizations, and innovations. To me, this was the fun stuff. This was play, not work.

While I was away, my company grew from $1 million to $20 million in four years, and from eight to eighty-five employees.

There's a big difference between being self-employed and being a business owner. Being self-employed feels like freedom until you realize that if you take time off, your business crumbles. To be a true business owner, make it so that you could leave for a year, and when you came back, your business would be doing better than when you left.

Make it anything you want

After your business has been up and running awhile, you'll hit an interesting crossroads.

Everyone assumes that as the owner of the company, you'll be the traditional CEO, having high-powered lunches with other high-powered CEOs and doing all the big business deals. But what if you don't like doing that? What if what you love the most is the solitude of the craft? Or talking to customers?

Never forget that you can make your role anything you want it to be. Anything you hate to do, someone else loves. So find that person and let her do it.

I loved sitting alone and programming, writing, planning, and inventing—thinking of ideas and making them happen. This makes me happy, not business deals or management. So I found someone who liked doing business deals and put him in charge of all that.

If you do this, you'll encounter a lot of pushback and misunderstanding, but who cares? You can't live someone else's expectation of a traditional business. You have to just do whatever you love the most, or you'll lose interest in the whole thing.

On a similar note, people also assume that you want to be big-big-big—as big as can be. But do you, really? Huge growth means lots of meetings, investors, bankers, media, and answering to others. It's quite far from the real core of the business.

Happiness is the real reason you're doing anything, right? Even if you say it's for the money, the money is just a means to happiness, isn't it? But what if it's proven that after a certain point, money doesn't create any happiness at all, but only headaches? You may be much happier as a $1 million business than a $1 billion business.

The funny thing is, I didn't want CD Baby to grow at all. Even from the start, I didn't want this website hobby to take away from my career as a musician, but it did. I didn't want it to have more than a couple of employees or outgrow my house, but it did. When I had twenty employees, I vowed to keep it that small, but customer demand kept growing, and I had to keep the customers happy. When I had fifty employees, I swore that was enough and we needed to curb this growth, but the business kept growing.

When people would ask, "What are you doing to grow your company?" I'd say, "Nothing! I'm trying to get it to stop growing! I don't like this. It's too big." They thought that was the weirdest thing. Doesn't every business want to be as big as possible?

No. Make sure you know what makes you happy, and don't forget it.

Trust, but verify

In 2005, CD Baby's main business was doing digital delivery of music to all the digital music retailers: iTunes, Amazon, Napster, Rhapsody, MSN, Yahoo!, and fifty more. This role was life-or-death important to the company because it was the main reason most of our new clients signed up. And there were lots of competitors in this field, so it was crucial that we did everything well.

I built a system that did most of the work, but it still required someone to run the outputs, connect hard drives, and ship them to the retailers. I hired a guy who seemed good. I sat side by side with him for a week, showing him the system, running it myself, and explaining how it all worked. He got it.

The key point was that we had to get every album delivered to every company, every week, no matter what. The guy I hired signed a contract with me that said, in huge letters, EVERY ALBUM, TO EVERY COMPANY, EVERY WEEK, NO MATTER WHAT. We talked a lot about how absolutely crucial that was— that it was really his only job requirement because it was that important. He signed and agreed.

His first few weeks, I watched closely to make sure everything was going well. It was. So I turned my attention back to other things.

A few months later, I started hearing a lot of complaints from musicians, saying that their music hadn't been sent to these companies. I logged in to the system to see what was wrong. It turns out that we hadn't sent any music to Napster, Amazon, and some other companies in months. Months!

I called the guy in charge of it and asked what was going on. He said, "Yeah, I've been really backed up. It's been really busy."

I said, "What's rule number one? The sole mission of your job?"

He said, "I know. Every album to every company every week no matter what. But I've been swamped. I just couldn't."

I flew up to Portland and let him go. I've never fired anyone so fast, but this was extreme. Our company's reputation was permanently damaged.

This job was so crucial to the company's survival that I decided to do it myself for a while—not just do it, but build a system that wouldn't let mistakes go unnoticed again. So for the next six months, I lived at the warehouse in Portland, and my sole job was digital deliveries. It took fifteen-hour days to catch up on months of backlog, but eventually we had a smooth system again.

I learned a hard lesson in hindsight: Trust, but verify.

Remember it when delegating. You have to do both.

Delegate,
but don't abdicate

Delegation doesn't come naturally to any of us. But I was trying really hard to be good at it. I knew how important it was to get into the delegation mind-set. I was trying to empower my employees—to let them know they could make decisions on their own, without me.

When they asked, "How should we organize all the rooms in the new office?" I said, "Any way you want to do it is fine."

When they asked, "Which health-care plan should we go with?" I said, "You guys choose. Take a vote. Whichever one you choose, I'll pay for."

When they asked, "Which profit-sharing plan should we go with?" I said, "You guys choose. Whatever you think is best."

A local magazine voted CD Baby "Best Place to Work" in the state of Oregon.

Six months later, my accountant called me and said, "Did you know that your employees set up a profit-sharing program?"

I said, "Yeah. Why?"

He said, "Did you know that they're giving all of the profits of the company back to themselves?"

Oops.

When I canceled the profit-sharing program, I became a

very unpopular guy. In our weekly company meetings, the general message from the employees was, "We need to get Derek out of here, so he stops telling us what to do. We don't need to answer to him! He needs to answer to us!"

Then I realized that there's such a thing as over-delegation. I had empowered my employees so much that I gave them all the power. After a complete communication breakdown, it was eighty-five people (my employees) against one (me). I became the scapegoat for all of their dissatisfaction.

I thought of trying to repair relationships with each of the eighty-five employees over hundreds of hours of talking. But if you've ever had a romance break up, you know that sometimes it's beyond repair.

So I considered firing everyone and hiring a whole new crew. I also considered shutting down the company entirely, since I wasn't enjoying this anymore. I even thought about a Willy Wonka move, in which I'd put five golden tickets into five CDs and then give the whole company to some lucky finder.

In the end, I did what was best for my clients and me: I retreated into solitude, staying at a friend's house in London, and focused entirely on programming some major new software features for CD Baby. I never saw or spoke to my employees again, never saw the office again.

I learned an important word: *abdicate*. To abdicate means to surrender or relinquish power or responsibility; this word is usually used when a king abdicates the throne or crown.

Lesson learned too late: Delegate, but don't abdicate.

How I knew I was done

I thought I would never sell CD Baby. When National Public Radio did a story about me in 2004, I said I'd stick it out until the end, and I meant it.

In 2007 I did a ground-up rewrite of the website from scratch. And man, it was beautiful code. The proudest achievement of my life so far is that rewritten software. Wonderfully organized, extensible, and efficient: the culmination of everything I'd learned about programming in ten years.

After a successful relaunch and Christmas rush, I was looking at my plans for 2008 and beyond. Every plan needed a huge effort for little reward, but all were required for future growth. I had broken the plans into about twenty projects of two to twelve weeks each, and I wasn't excited about any of them. I'd taken CD Baby far beyond my goals, and I realized I had no big vision for its being much else.

The next week, I got calls from three companies, each asking if I'd be interested in selling. I said no, as usual, since I'd been giving the same answer for ten years.

But just to be open-minded, that weekend I opened my diary and started answering the question, "What if I sold?" I had done this a few times in previous years, but the answer had always been, "No way! There's so much more I want to do! This is my baby. I can't stop now!"

This time it was different. I thought about how nice it'd be to not have eighty-five employees and all that responsibility. I wrote about how nice it'd be to get outside a bit and feel free of all that. I got excited about all the cool new projects I could do instead.

I realized that the bigger learning and growing challenge for me was letting go, not staying on.

Surprised by this, I asked Seth Godin's advice. All he said was, "If you care, sell." (I think his point was that my lack of enthusiastic vision was doing a disservice to my clients. It'd be better for everyone if I put the company in more motivated hands that could help them all grow.)

I called Jared Rose, my business coach, and asked him to grill me about this big decision. "What other ways can you achieve the freedom you want, without selling?" he asked me. After an hour of questions like this, we both came to the conclusion that I was really done.

As with any breakup, graduation, or move, you emotionally disconnect, and it all feels as if it's in the distant past. I felt like I was already on the highway with a little box of stuff, moving cross-country, with my old home long gone, never to be seen again. By the end of that day, I was no longer derek@cdbaby.com.

Unfortunately, as with a divorce, the paperwork took another seven months. I let two companies bid, and ended up choosing the one that bid lower but understood my clients better.

It was never about the money. The decision was done in that one introspective day of writing in my diary and talking with my mentors. Afterward, I was completely unconflicted and knew it was the right decision.

I went to bed that night (January 18, 2008) and slept longer than I had in months. Then I woke up full of detailed ideas for my next company, but that's a different story.

I've been asked a few times by other entrepreneurs, "How do you know when it's time to sell?"

My answer is, "You'll know." But I hope this detailed story describes how it will feel.

Why I gave my company to charity

Kurt Vonnegut and Joseph Heller were at a party at a billionaire's extravagant estate. Kurt said, "Wow! Look at this place! This guy has everything!" Joseph said, "Yes, but I have something he'll never have.... Enough."

When I decided to sell CD Baby, I already had enough. I live simply. I don't own a house, a car, or even a TV. The less I own, the happier I am. The lack of stuff gives me the priceless freedom to live anywhere anytime.

So I didn't need or even want the money from the sale of the company. I just wanted to make sure I had enough for a simple, comfortable life. The rest should go to music education because that's what made such a difference in my life.

I created a charitable trust called the Independent Musicians Charitable Remainder Unitrust. When I die, all of its assets will go to music education. But while I'm alive, it pays out 5 percent of its value per year to me. A few months before the sale, I transferred all the CD Baby assets into the trust. It was irrevocably gone. It was no longer mine. It all belonged to the charitable trust.

Then, when Disc Makers bought CD Baby, they bought it

not from me but from the trust, turning it into $22 million cash to benefit music education.

It's not that I'm altruistic. I'm sacrificing nothing. I've just learned what makes me happy. And doing it this way made me the happiest.

I get the deeper happiness of knowing that the lucky streak I've had in my life will benefit tons of people—not just me. I get the pride of knowing I did something smart and irreversible before I could change my mind. I get the safety of knowing I won't be the target of wrongful lawsuits, since I have very little net worth. I get the unburdened freedom of having it out of my hands so I can't do something stupid.

But most of all, I get the constant priceless reminder that I have enough.

You make your perfect world

I started CD Baby focused on the importance of making a dream-come-true perfect world for musicians. Along the way I learned the importance of making my business a dream come true for myself, too.

Business is as creative as the fine arts. You can be as unconventional, unique, and quirky as you want. A business is a reflection of the creator.

▶ Some people want to be billionaires with thousands of employees. Some people want to work alone.

▶ Some want as much profit as possible. Some want as little profit as possible.

▶ Some want to be in Silicon Valley with Fortune 500 customers. Some want to be anonymous.

No matter which goal you choose, there will be lots of people telling you you're wrong.

Just pay close attention to what excites you and what drains you. Pay close attention to when you're being the real you and when you're trying to impress an invisible jury.

Even if what you're doing is slowing the growth of your business—if it makes you happy, that's OK. It's your choice to remain small.

You'll notice that as my company got bigger, my stories about it were less happy. That was my lesson learned. I'm happier with five employees than with eighty-five, and happiest working alone.

Whatever you make, it's your creation, so make it your personal dream come true.

Contact me anytime

The coolest people I meet are the ones who find me through something I've written. So if you made it this far, please go to **http://sivers.org** and e-mail me to say hello. I get really inspired by people's questions, so feel free to ask me anything, or just tell me what you're working on. I'm glad to help.

Acknowledgments

Every one of these people took a couple of hours to carefully read a draft of this book and suggest detailed improvements. Whether a changed word or a huge structural change, each one of their suggestions made the book better for everyone else. So huge thanks to: Aaron Goldfarb, Adam Di Stefano, Adam Seawright, Ahmed Adam, Aisha Yusaf, Alex Wagenheim, Amy Osajima, Ashish Dixit, Balarko Banerjee, Ben Scherrey, Ben Unger, Benjamin Hinnant, Bernadette Jiwa, Bill West, Brice Royer, Catherine Louis, Chew Lin Kay, Christoph Vonihr, Craig Millman, David Isaacson, David Norton, Debi Miller, Derek Mounce, Drasko Raicevic, Drew Jarrod, Elomar Nascimento dos Santos, Eric Hebert, Erin Sinogba, Fredrik Hertzberg, Gen Berthault, Greg Arney, Harry Hollander, Heidi Ohlander, Ian Alas, Ian Clifford, Ilse de Jong, J. J. Vicars, James Shvarts, Jean Synodinos, Jim Glinn, Jim Kitson, Joao Vincient Lewis, Joaquin Paolo, Joe Baldwin, Jose Castro-Frenzel, Julie Yount, Karol Gajda, Kohan Ikin, Laurentiu Nicolae, Marc Plotkin, Marco Bosca, Marie Angell, Mark Lengies, Mark Needham, Matt Butson, Melissa Rebronja, Michael Cloin, Mike Rubini, Miles Carroll, Neil Davidson, Noah Litvin, Noel Sequeira, Pallavi Shrivastava, Patrick Ranahan, Patrick Smith, Paul Adams, Paul Kenny, Paul Sedkowski, Ravi Rao, Reinder de Vries, Renee Quail, Rick Goetz, Rob

ACKNOWLEDGMENTS

Szabo, Ross Hill, Rowan Simpson, Roy Naim, Roy Povarchik, Ryan Irelan, Scott Honsberger, Sean Tierney, She Hui Felix Leong, Serdar Usta, Stephen Bové, Tanya Mulkidzhanova, Tan Yew Wei, Thad Moody, Tony Brigmon, Tyler Quinn, Tynan, and Victor Johnson.

11/15/17